The Horny People's Guide to

Sexercise

Adult Humor
by Juan Carman Carlos

Illustrated
IN STICK FIGURES
Anatomically Correct

The Horny People's Guide to Sexercise
Or Killing Two Birds with 2 Rocks, a Stick & a Loose O-Ring in Stick Figures

iUniverse books may be ordered through booksellers or by contacting:

iUniverse
1663 Liberty Drive
Bloomington, IN 47403
www.iuniverse.com
1-800-Authors (1-800-288-4677)

ISBN: 978-1-5320-7314-4 (sc)
ISBN: 978-1-5320-7315-1 (e)

Library of Congress Control Number: 2019911321

Print information available on the last page.

iUniverse rev. date: 08/08/2019

Forward

OFFICIAL WARNING

If you are ready for sex,
Have an agreeable partner/s,
(we don't care who, what or
how many) and you've done all
of your prerequisites,
DO NOT BEGIN
READING THIS BOOK.
YOUR MOOD MAY BE DESTROYED
BY LAUGHTER.

Acknowledgments

Thanks to:
Carmen for the years of love & Passion
All the women in my life since
And God for all those years without
sex which made me crazy enough
to write this book.

Author's Note!

This entire book came to me in a dream in the middle of the night in I think 1997. I woke up laughing so hard that I just had to write it down. All I could find was a stack of half sheets of old computer paper with the holes on the side plus a blue pen a red pen and a purple pen. After folding several sheets in half I wrote and drew as fast as I could in tiny script trying not to forget any of it.

About 2 am I could not write any more. I was too tired to try to draw elephants. So I had to finish the rest of it in the morning. And I added the glossary of (5th grade) terms. It took over a year to translate - decipher the scribbled long hand (for example the illustration on page 41, *"Where the Hell are the Batteries,"* enlarged and touched up is still hard to read), and then type it into a readable form. There was a celebration with martinis at this stage, but the stick figures were not included.

It has taken another 17 years to do the stick figures and to get enough courage to copyright and attempt to publish. The stick figures vary from copies from the original, to ones altered by the computer, to hand drawn replacements, to 'scissored' color separations from the scanner. I hope all these efforts are worth your while!

The author

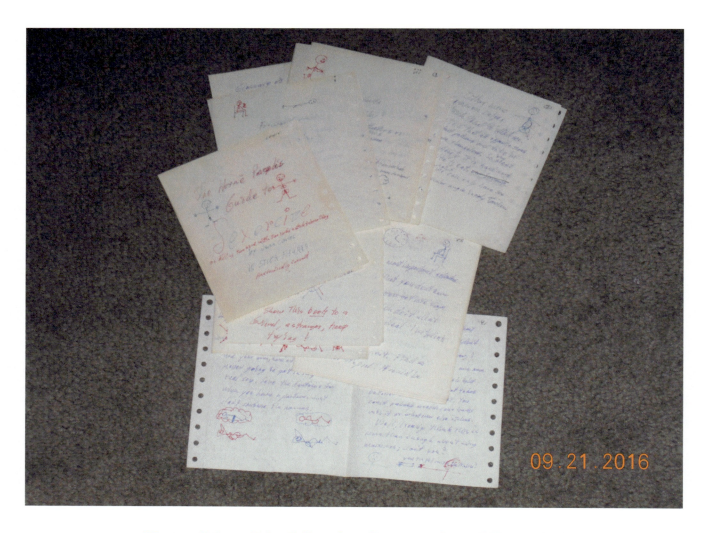

Photo of the original, hand-written version of 'Sexercise'

Table of Contents

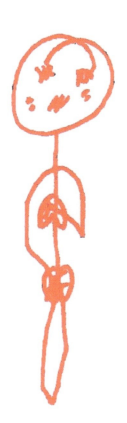

Chapter Uno

Why?

But Hesh Doesn't Know

Because Women Know that all men are Stupid. A few men have also become aware of that fact and all men know that women haven't got a brain in their heads. (No one will admit to this quote)

Why are there gyms full of people on exercise & weight lifting machines, doing exercises, found jogging at 5 a.m. and investing bookoo dollars on equipment and special clothes?

YOU guessed it. SEX!

We want to be more attractive, i.e. appealing to the weaker sex--that's women's muscular strength to males and men's intelligence to females.

Body Building

Some people get confused and think that exercise is fun! They end up with strange looking bulges on their bodies and sometimes even forget about sex altogether, except perhaps in the mirror. Their genitals seem to somehow get lost in the competition of shapes and bulges. Remember, the whole point of this pain and misery was to attract a partner for *SEX*, yours or somebody else's.

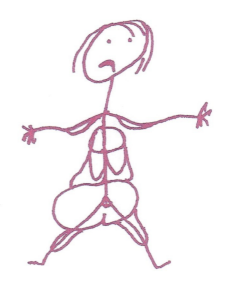

Other
More
Common
Bulges

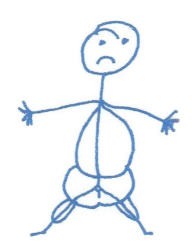

These tend to inhibit sex.

I've been told that all opposite sexes want perfect bodies (on their partners) and to be in perfect shape themselves. So, why aren't we?

Obviously it is hard work and we like to eat. So what, if we can only have sex at one particular angle which is nearly impossible for humans or even orangutans!

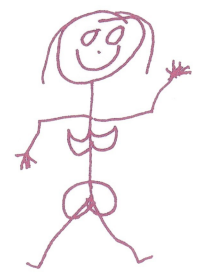

Sexercise
Can change
Your Life!

And, You can look like this, feel great (especially when you feel each other), improve your health and be HAPPY!

So, what is Sexercise, you may ask. For those of you who are mentally challenged it is simply combining exercise with sex! Duuh!

Chapter Duo

Calisthenics vs Aerobics

If you're not over 50, you probably have never even heard of Calisthenics. That is what high school PE (physical exercise) was called.

If you are over 50, you should know that aerobics will not kill you. Even if you are afraid of heights and feel like you have taken your last breath, such calamities are pretty rare, I think.

But, and other parts of your body may be stretched, pulled and twisted way beyond normal. However, these

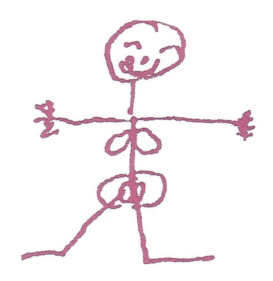

a e r o b i c exercises appear to be very sexually stimulating, which may explain why women like to do them.

So, Why don't men like to do them and why do women like to do aerobics with lots of other women in a group?

It seems that men are embarrassed to be seen sexually excited in a _group_ of women. Especially when there is no place to have one on one sex without an audience and by the time you are finished 'aerobicizing' you're too exhausted anyway.

I think the women's problems are partly genetic. Besides, it is well known through the research of Randy Travis that women like to sit around and talk about men, which makes the men even more nervous when the girls congregate.

Marathon  Sex

can sometimes replace sexercise. But, it usually only lasts a few years in a marriage or relationship and fails due to conflicting schedules, children, exhaustion, etc.

Sexercise really is a better solution. It combines the best parts of aerobics and calisthenics - -and you can even leave off the s and tell your children that you are doing your exercises and lock the door anytime of the day or night especially if your child is likely to walk in on you (which is what occurred when I was little).

Not knowing the proper term at the tender age of four or five I said, "Excuse me Mother and Father, I didn't know that you were doing your exercises," and walked out thinking nothing more of it. My Dad told the story over and over as I was growing up much to my anguish and embarrassment.

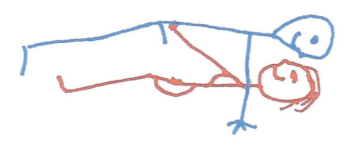

Another big plus is time. No one complains about a five minute exercise program! "In just 5 minutes a day with our machine," they advertise, "You can have a perfect body." Bull_____! You are in a hurry to get into shape, so you can have sex. You workout for hours and are too tired for sex, get frustrated and throw the damned machine away.

With sexercise you can squeeze in a few minutes here or there and both have a smile on your face. You can even extend your *work-ins* to 30 minutes or longer. *Now you've just been given a new word-phrase. Who in their right mind wants to work OUT of sex! So, let's <u>work-in</u> to sex!* You with me so far?

I think that you are ready for chapter 3. So, turn the page.

You're going to be fabulous at this. Just look how well you follow instructions.

Chapter 3

The Two-Some

Note: This was supposed to be A Bi-lingual book, but, the only Other words I learned were, "Dame um besso". And I don't Even know how to spell it.

The 2-some of course is the preferred method of sexercise. There may, will probably, well, I might get around to writing a chapter for solo sexercise, that is, if I don't find a partner.

And for you same sex couples, you'll just have to improvise. Besides, you are probably accustomed to making adjustments.

One point I would like to make for you solo's is this, if you only use one arm, hand, & or finger, you're never going to get in shape for *real* sex. Besides, you might become muscle bound or even get carpel tunnel disease from excessive restricted motion.

Also, save the fantasies for when you have a partner and really need them. And, if you tend to talk out loud, don't confuse the names!

Probably the most important advantage to sexercise is that you don't have to wait until you get into shape to have sex. You do it all at once! What a deal, "I'm telink ya!"

So, what's next?

Find a partner stupid. It could be your spouse, your girlfriend, boyfriend, your better half, your mate, your neighbor *(assuming hesh is over 18 and not younger than your children unless they live far, far away and you don't have any money.)*

You could try the personals. These people obviously want sex and can't find it. They may be out of shape too, which explains why they have to advertise.

If you are in need of an example, you can use mine as a guide.

Slightly plump little old man who is 53 that either has a mild case of adult ADD or is just a little lazy, stupid and crazy. He is a little in debt, has a sports car with a broken engine and is looking for a wealthy widow to whisk him away to exotic and romantic places. She only needs to be nice to look at and have a pleasant disposition. It would be nice if she likes my grandkids, but that's not a requirement. It would also help if she tolerates the crazy car brothers and things classical. 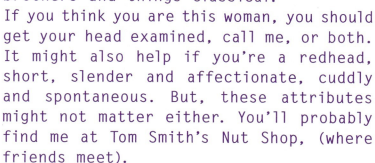 If you think you are this woman, you should get your head examined, call me, or both. It might also help if you're a redhead, short, slender and affectionate, cuddly and spontaneous. But, these attributes might not matter either. You'll probably find me at Tom Smith's Nut Shop, (where friends meet).

Note: This is an old ad. I'm not 53 anymore.

When I went to place this ad in the local newspaper they told me that it would cost me $45. They didn't need humor that badly and now Tom Smith's, a coffee shop, bar and restaurant, is closed, too. So this may not help at all.

Wanna have some fun sex or what!

Prostitutes might go along with it since they've dealt with kinky sex requests before yours. But, they'd have to be pretty stupid to do it for nothing. And, if you have to pay for it, just have sex and skip the sexercise. Also, if you were really serious about getting in shape, you would not be reading this book and would park five miles away from the brothel and walk every day.

Anyway, this is your problem and for the interest of continuing this book, I'll assume that you have found a partner- - of the opposite sex- - even if I haven't.

People come in all shapes and sizes. Some people don't physically fit very well together. This is very unfortunate, if this is your case. And if you happen to be married to each other, you have funked up Royally, i.e. you're an RF (a Royal Funkup).

Note: The computer says the past tense of the F word should be spelled with an <u>n</u> instead of a <u>c</u>. There is no alternative for Funkup. End of note.

However, the great one has given humans a mind with which they can conquer just about anything. In your case fantasy may be the best antidote.

I hope you singles are paying attention, because, if you should become an RF, this is where you'll <u>need</u> fantasies.

    Another idea is to give each other a photo of what you looked like at 18 of yourself or perhaps of someone else, especially if it is a nude picture. That is, unless you look better with clothes on. (Then definitely use someone else's picture.)

    Speaking of clothes, the preferred routine is without, clothes that is. Who wants to call 911 to have a zipper removed?

    A certain part of male bodies do need covering now days, if you know what I mean. Or not, if you're an ancient Catholic and want lots of children.

Some situations may call for certain types of garments which can also be very useful. Something to support certain appendages that stretch and stretch and stretch from being periodically over filled and bounced too much would be very helpful.

Not your penis stupid. It is just a sponge which gets a little bit bigger when it's filled with fluid, but it won't stretch. You've been trying to stretch it for years to no avail.

A suggestion here might be in order. There is a place in Hollywood that sells bras that have holes for your raspberries. (Men are really turned on by the sight of bare nipples. Actually they are really turned on by the sight of bare anything.)

Hand holding gets sweaty.
Try holding something else!

They also have support garments for bottoms with openings in the crotch for you know what. (If you don't know what, you are either too young to be reading this book or you should be reading a how to sex manual.)

Guys, if it won't get hard or it flops too much, you might consider a <u>Jock strap</u>. It can easily be pulled aside at the right moment for some of the bouncyer (this is not a new word, I think it came from Eeyore) sexercise routines. Actually something in a clear or transparent would be nice. They can help to keep your <u>rubbers</u> on too.

Now let's get back to the girls. (That's one of the names men call you when you're not around. They only call you ladies when they want to impress you.) If you are impatient and can't wait for the package in the mail, you can always get out the scissors and cut holes in your bra and panties. I like red ones.

Don't under any circumstances allow any men to have scissors or any other sharp instrument in this situation! They tend to get excited and we wouldn't want any accidents to happen.

Put the item on, mark it, and _TAKE IT OFF BEFORE YOU CUT._ This is not a program for masochists. It is for people too damn lazy to exercise.

A better solution to bouncing is to have your partner hold the little critters, monsters or whatever you want to

"Breathing is essential inhale, Swallow, exhale!"

call them while you jump up and down, do deep knee bends, deep throat, deep penetration, (this is getting too deep for me).

You really don't need any other equipment besides your little play things. But, if you have some exercise equipment, ways to adapt them will be covered in a later chapter.

You may want to experiment with different routines by using front to front, front to back, back to front, or back to back. (This last one takes a little ingenuity.)

If you haven't been watching the little stick figures, you are probably bored to, well, why did you buy this book anyway?

By the way, whether or not you do have money or are famous, you can take a tip from GOD i.e. George, a 90 year old man who wrote an exercise book for seniors, or an old lion named Clarence. If you follow their example you'll have a female on each side to hold you up for whatever you have in mind.

I'm sorry! I couldn't find the Book!

This should probably be classified as group sex, but since they are only assisting, they don't count.)

And remember, the exercises were for every day or something like that. I read the book a long time ago, but I remember the girls in the pictures were cute.

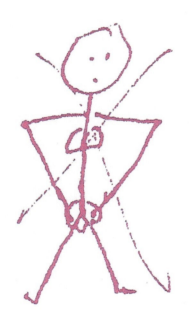

Chapter 4

Goin Solo
Not Yet

Show this book to
a friend, a stranger.
Just keep trying!

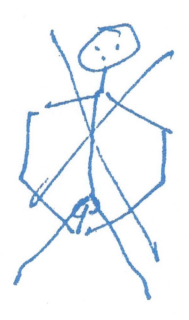

Chapter 5

Group Sexercise

At first I thought this idea was a little too kinky. But then, Clarence got me thinking. You remember Clarence, the old blind lion? His pride (Female lions) would take turns standing at his side holding him up while he did his duty with one of the other female lions.

That's quite a foursome and, I bet, a lot more fun than golf.

By now you may have gathered that I haven't had a lot of experience in this area. So, if you find any of these routines unsatisfactory, you've been warned. And, don't bother to sue me because it's obvious that I don't know what the hell I'm doing.

(Well it's after 2 am and I'm too tired from writing and laughing for sex. So, goodnight.)

End of the first half. Coming next --Elephants.

YOU WILL HAVE TO PROVIDE YOUR OWN HALF TIME ENTERTAINMENT!

 *2nd installment*

Chapter 5 continued

As I promised in the first installment, I will tell you all about how Elephants do it. Well, actually I didn't promise. But, if I do, DON'T believe it!

Anyway, when I was a little boy my Grandmother traveled around the world playing piano and composing music. She spent a year in Ceylon and India around 1949 and when she returned she played and sang the story songs about the Elephants and monkeys that she had written. She also gave me a child's book about Elephants, too! So, this is an OK thing, and I still have the book! Plus having read nature magazines and watched shows about Elephants on TV, you can see that I'm pretty much an expert on Elephants.

　　Besides that, my Dad had a complete set of Playboy magazines up until he died in 1990. And of course there is an X rated part to this.

　　Anyway, right in the middle of my dream I'm watching a program when they start talking about sex--Elephant sex. Then along comes this huge bull Elephant with a <u>trunk in back</u>. His thing was so enormous that it drug on the ground!

　　Next they show him chasing this little teenage Elephant. She makes lots of squeals and other noises. Being in heat only once every four years, she makes only a half hearted effort to get away, and tries not to look at his log.

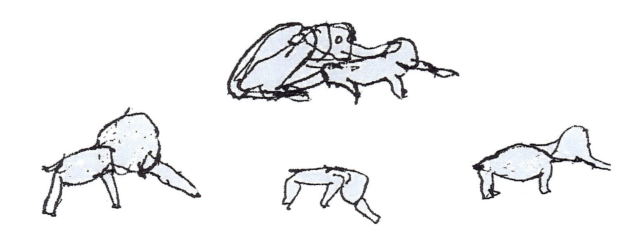

All the while the whole herd is within viewing distance!
The whole point to this story, beside the fact that I like Elephants and sex, is that, if you have a huge dick that nearly drags on the ground, you might be willing to do group sexercise since you have something to show off. That would be especially true if you could only use it every four years.
You'd probably be better off selling the video though.

Well, I think that is about enough about Groups! I bet you're glad about that.

Note: I'm sorry if I have offended anyone, but, now you know why I made that crack about "write your own book." It is plain to see that you could do a lot better job for sure!

Chapter 5.5

If Billy Gates can do
Fractions, so can I.

Weight Loss & Specific Muscle Development

First of all, I think we had better have a short anatomy lesson. See pictures.

Remember, Guys and Gals there is no muscle in a p. It is just a sponge. Your muscles are in your head, so to speak.

Now that we have that straight, there won't be any penile exercises to lose weight nor to increase your p size!

Now as for you ladies, I've never heard of a p being too small at the opening. But, if you do have a problem, there is a sure cure. It only takes nine months or so, and can be repeated. Artificial methods or even a surrogate can be had to begin the process. However, there are long term side effects--*CHILDREN!*

It would be a lot easier to find a partner with a smaller size. Believe me there are lots of them around.

Note: I initially wrote smaller partner, but, I was afraid you might misunderstand me!

As most people with any sense already know that to stop eating all the time and to walk a lot is the best way to lose weight. Since you've already ignored that, I'll have to come up with something else.

My personal method is to deliver newspapers. It is great in the summer. I go out every day early in the morning with a heavy sack of papers. This builds up my back, stomach, butt, and leg muscles as well as my shoulders and <u>right arm</u>. At this rate I'm going to become unbalanced to the right! (A picture of Gingrich just went through my head. What a scary thought.)

Anyway, in the winter my butt and dick would get *cold as* _____*!* (I'm trying to clean this up a little.)

Sexercise could cure this problem. A warm female hand to rub my b and another warm hand to hold my dick while I stick my spare hand in her jane would solve all the cold problems.

Note: since this is sort of a primer on sexercise, don't you think it appropriate to use dick and jane?

If there were two women, It could be sort of like helping George or Clarence, and they would each still have a hand to talk with.

Wow! Rn't I smart.

Maybe you've heard of the Kegel exercise or the pubocoxic muscle. If you're serious about that stuff, take an anatomy class.

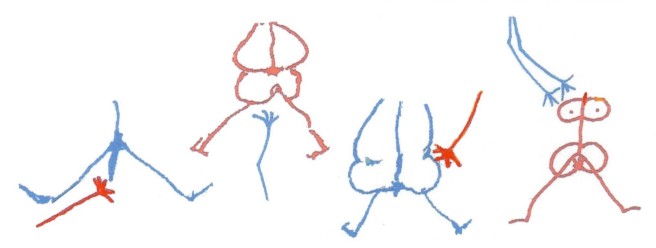

When you are doing your sexercises tense your muscle area that is being supported, touched, rubbed, etc. by your partner. This doesn't necessarily remove the fat, but it does tend to help you to hold it in place. Specific areas needing attention are butt, stomach, thighs, upper arms, and hips. This is something that you can do together every day. What a wonderful way to tone up those problem areas and enjoy all the foreplay.

This might be a great place to practice your stick figures!

Chapter 6
Machines & How to Adapt Them

Many machines are already ready for sexercise. You just both get on at once! Examples are the ski and walking machines. You just stride in step and hold on to whatever is handy.

Of course the stationary exercise bike offers great possibilities for sexercising. Seat your partner in your lap, on the handle bars facing you, or on the bars leaning forward.

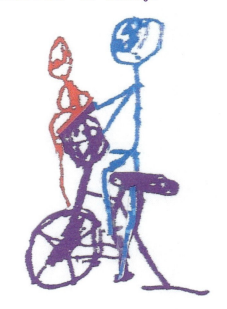

Next is the rowing machine. Your partner can stand in front of you, sit in front of you, or get down on all fours in front of you.

You people are just going to have to use your imagination here! Remember, to trade places too.

This probably won't work either. So, if you videotape this, you can watch if after a bit and have a really good belly laugh watching your handiwork.

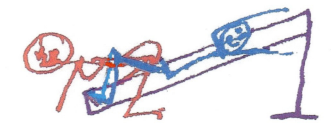

I don't really know much about exercise machines because I don't believe in exercise. However, I understand that some women use a little flash light like portable thing that takes batteries and shakes a lot. You could probably scratch your backs with it or whatever else itches.

Well, I really think that this is more than enough about machines. Don't You?

Try your luck at drawing
stick figures

Chapter 7

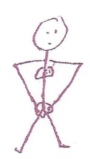

Which is actually Chapter 4

*But you really needed to
keep trying!*

Well here it is at last the chapter on SOLO SEXERCISE--which really isn't sex at all because <u>real</u> sex is intercourse between a male and a female (and I don't mean talking) -- which most of you have been anxiously waiting for.

The easiest sexercise for singling, (rhymes with ding a ling), is running in place while pumping your hole or your pole. This is a great one for the bath room. While you run a hot shower you can get the effect of getting all steamed up with a partner. Or you could sing one of your old dirty fraternity or sorority songs too, if that helps. If you're not a frat rat or a sorority brat, (I know that's misspelled but that's the way my dad pronounced it), you could try one of your old summer camp songs. Failing that, you'll just have to make something up or YODELL! If you do any singing at all you can probably forget about ever finding a partner.

Now that you woke up the whole neighborhood, I think that we should try something else.

How about jumping Jacks or jumping Jills, pump and jump, jump and pump, etc. Or perhaps, you could see how high you can bounce your little things.

Just think how much better it would be if you had a partner. You Jacks and Jills could be jumping and humping each other. Now, wouldn't that be more fun?

I'm really getting tired of trying to help you people. Besides, you are so lazy that you probably just lay there and only move your hand or finger anyway.

Well, here's one last idea. You know that a picture is worth a thousand words. Now a really good picture or maybe several could be worth thousands of orgasms.

So here's what you do. Take five of your favorite pictures. (I especially like the ones with the big nipples and the crotch shots). Place them around you just out of reach. Pin one to the ceiling, too. Now twist, fold and stretch your body trying to reach out and touch each of your favorite pin-ups. Once your own little parts start responding, you're ready for the next sexercise.

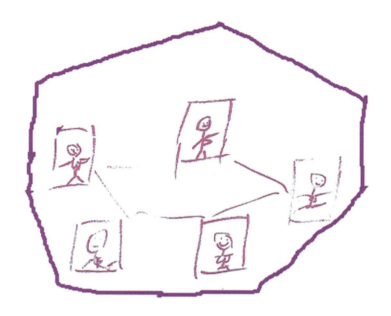

Pick up your pictures and place them in the 5 corners of your house or apartment. If you have ever had physical therapy in a hospital or nursing facility, you know how they like to do 5 reps of everything. 5 Reps means you do the same exercise over and over and over and over and over again.

Look, if you don't understand some of these words, just look them up in the glossary. (Go to the back of the book and turn the pages backwards.)

You're probably used to doing things backwards anyway, which may explain why you haven't got a partner yet!

(Insert picture)

Now you've probably lost all of your "swellingness" or "wetness" whichever is your gender condition. So, you may have to stare at one of your pictures and rub something a little--5 reps maximum. Are you ready now? OK. Now run to the next picture and do 5 more reps--one, two, three, four, five. (Therapists always count out loud for you just in case you broke your brain when you fell and broke your hip.) Now run to the next picture and do 5 reps--counting out loud, one, two, three, four, five. Keep doing this going to all 5 pictures and repeating the cycle until you're satisfied, or are completely exhausted.

If you do this sexercise, you'll really start to see some improvement in your health, maybe lose some weight plus you'll get really *FAST*, if you know what I mean. That is, if you don't stop to eat donuts in the kitchen.

Well, good luck and save me a maple bar!

Appendix A

List of Sexercises in No apparent order at all

(Remember to keep your outer rubbers, inner rubbers, and whatever else you need to prevent complications handy.)

1. Jumping Jacks/Jumping Jills-
     I think when they fell down (on all fours probably) Jill broke something. But, I don't think it was her crown. I think it was her hymen. I suppose it only happened once or maybe twice, who knows?

2. Push n Pull Ins/Pull n Push Outs-
     (The guy part is listed first for any of you who care). This is mostly a 2 person Sexercise! (Otherwise it is just plain old masturbation). This is done just like a pushup except with somebody under you when you fall. Remember to keep your feet and

body straight. You can get up on your fingertips, if you think that YOU are MACHO, but don't try to clap your hands. You might hurt someone.

3. Squats or Ups & Downs-

For a fynatious?? *(After 20 years I still can't figure out what this word is. -the author)* Jack lies down while Jill stands straddling his mid-section and squats down while Jack tries to direct his little thing at her target. Just for fun you could draw circles around it with some old lipstick. Jill can bounce around a little, if she likes. Then she must return to the standing position or it's considered cheating or just plain old sex. Remember only 5 reps at a time.

In Squat ups Jill leans over something while Jack assumes a squat position behind her with one hand on her derriere (for balance only) and the other hand on his little thing for guidance. Jack rises to a standing position or as close as possible depending on Jill's bottom to floor elevation, i.e. height. This is why elevator shoes were invented, I think. He can bounce around a little, but remember no more than 5 reps. Both Jack and Jill can also do the ankle and foot sexercise by raising their heels about 4 inches. That's probably all he's got anyway!

4. Kiss ups

One partner stands with legs slightly apart while the other from a prone position sits up and gives a kiss, or whatever to the most interesting thing you come into contact with. This is limited to 5 for each sit up which are up to your limit????

5. Leap Frog

If you do this right, you usually fall down and get your little things tangled up.

6. Hanky Panky

Is sung to the tune of Hokey Pokey and sort of like aerobics. Jack jumps forward (after dropping a hanky for Jill to bend over)

47

behind Jill and puts his little P in Jill's P to make a Q. This is how we got "Watching our P's and Q's.

7. Seek and Hide (at least some running is expected here)

Jill runs. Jack chases until he catches her. Jack finds a place in Jill to hide his little thing. This *must* be a place to Jill's liking. You can also use whatever you like for this activity. Only 5 reps at a time though.

8. Chin ups

Jack can sit down for this one. Jill stands and holds Jack by the chin and pulls him up to her Bs and counts to 5 and then sets him down. Jack can do whatever Jill wants him to do with his hands and mouth.

If Jill gets tired of standing, she can sit and Jack can lift her up. If he goes for the boobs, he might suffer from back strain. The best part is the rest period when whichever one is sitting can play with whatever meets the eye. Remember only 5 reps. The rest periods are excluded from this requirement.

9. By now you should be able to make up some of your own Sexercise routines. Or you should be in such great shape that you can just have normal sex!

Note: It may be advisable to get a doctor's advice before attempting any of these ridiculous activities. None of them have ever been tried before to my knowledge. Besides, maybe a few doctors might want to buy the book (for medicinal purposes of course).

Appendix G

Glossary *of Strange & Weird Words*

These are words that you've probably never heard of and will probably never see again unless I write a sequel.

Somewhat in order of appearance

HORNY = A feeling that you want to have a lot of sex a lot of the time.

HESH = A way to say he and she at the same time.

SEXERCISE = This is just basically athletic sex.

ANATOMICALLY CORRECT = For you morons this means the blue ones are males and the red ones are females.

UNO = A weird way of saying one and "You Know" at the same time.

BOOKOO = This means a lot more money than a person can afford.

MARATHON SEX = And, you thought you knew this one. Ha! An hour doesn't cut it. You have to go all night at least. This normally only happens at high school, college, or Navy wild parties and on rare occasions on honeymoons.

WORK-INS = This is the old putting P in P to make a Q act.

2-SOME = This usually means a man and a woman. But, I've seen men on a dance floor with brooms and even inflatable dolls before, so your guess is as good as mine.

FUCK = I just wanted to see if I could get this past the censors. Did you know that this is a very old word and didn't come from the beatniks in the 50's? What a SURPRISE!

BETTER HALF = This usually refers to someone with whom you live and with whom you have sex. It is something you say to make that person think that hesh is smarter than you because yesterday you said hesh was a complete nincompoop and everyone knows what that is.

PROSTITUTES = These people have the most admired jobs in the world and everyone is so jealous that they try to make them look really bad.

ROYAL FUNKUP = The only socially acceptable form of the word <u>fuck</u>.

BOUNCYER = You can use your imagination or read Winnie the Pooh books to get this one.

RUBBERS = These are not the kind that go on your feet. You'll find them in machines in the bathrooms of cheap bars & motels, or on your doctor when you go in for a pap smear or dental exam.

LITTLE CRITTERS = This is another term for Ps and Bs, love handles, or varied sizes of loose flesh.

LITTLE PLAYTHINGS = These are mostly Ps and Bs.

PRIDE = What male lions get after fighting off all the rest of the studs on their turf, plus, a short life span and a big smile.

GOLF = A stupid game guys play where you try to get a ball in a bunch of holes. Everyone knows it's easier to put your pole in the hole than your balls. Strangely enough women play the game too. At least they get to walk in simulated country.

IMMORAL = This refers to the things that we shouldn't do, but, do anyway. Or, at least we wish we could do.

PENCIL = Another word for a man's P.

ANALISTS = People who like to poke around in the little pond.

POLE = Another word for a man's P.

HOLE = Another word for a woman's P.

PUMP = Another word for describing how to put his P in her P. Sometimes used to describe mono sex.

HUMP = Same as above, but doesn't include mono sex. Also, what the dog is trying to do when he wraps around your leg.

SWELLINGNESS = This refers to when your Sponge is full and at attention.

ORGASM = That's when everything gets sticky and you get a big smile.

Ps = This refers to the most important parts of the male and female anatomies.

Bs = This refers to the second most important parts of the male and primarily female anatomies.

Medicinal Note!

This is on the order of "Having a drink for medicinal purposes." If you have a friend or happen to know a female who is quite often bitchy, complains a lot and is pretty much a <u>pain</u>. (This is a key word in medical circles, well, at least in poor underpaid nursing assistant gab sessions, otherwise called cigarette breaks). This sub-scription to restore the chemical-hormonal balance may help.

Sx

Juan C. Carlos MUD
Dr. of the John

Testosterone

Insert one or two doses two to three times
per day to combat bitchiness. Use a live, firm,
flexible applicator.
The applicator may need to be rubbed a little
and lubricated first.

Take standard precautions to avoid complications.

For bitchy men simply apply hormonal-rich honey from her P pot for instant relief.

About the Author

Juan Carman Carlos, (not his real name; would you admit to writing this book if you lived in a small town?), was raised in a small western town near Idaho to an artist mother and playboy father. He finished high school, then on to college in California.

This was followed by four years in the Navy where he was sent to Washington D.C., San Francisco, and Viet Nam on a seven month "Kiddie Cruise" with nearly seven weeks in ports such as Hong Kong, China; Sasebo, Yokosuka, Tokyo and Kyoto, Japan; Manilla, Philippines; and Pearl Harbor, Hawaii. Then he flew back to San Francisco.

Juan then went to the alter where he married Carmen, a Spanish beauty, went to work, (at over 53 jobs at last count), went to the same hospital building three times, (for the births of his three beautiful children all born at different hospitals--the name changed), went to the army butcher, (figured out what caused the children and had a vasectomy), went to divorce court, went to her funeral, went crazy, went to Mr. Mother on the job training program, went crazier, survived and went to see his grandchildren, (the very best part of all). And with nursing assistant training he helped his ailing Mother and many old family friends before they died.

Perhaps now you can see how he came to write this silly little book. And 20 years later has decided to publish it nearly four years after the love of his life died of cancer.